Spiral

OTHER BOOKS BY LYNDA LA ROCCA

In the Shortness of My Days

The Stillness Between

Spiral

Poems by

Lynda La Rocca

Liquid Light Press

Premium Chapbook First Edition

ISBN: 978-0-9836063-4-5

Liquid Light Press

poetry that speaks to the heart

www.liquidlightpress.com

Photos by Stephen M. Voynick
Cover Design by M. D. Friedman

Spiral

to all of them

I Am (1)

I am a girl who was never wanted,
a woman with eyes ringed by blue flame.
I am a sparrow with wings that are broken,
a serpent who lets the poor, maimed creature live.
I am a stone that cannot reach water,
a bright knife, an arrow that plunges through flesh.
I am a girl who was sometimes needed,
a servant who carries a basket of bread.
I am a cream-colored rose in the garden,
a pink worm that gnaws at the root in the dark.
I am a raindrop that mirrors the sunlight,
a sharp grain of sand at the heart of the pearl.
I am a girl who was always the last one,
I am a tortoise, a tortoise am I;
on my black shell I balance
the wobbly world.

Spiral

In the sky will be seen a fire
dragging a trail of sparks. — Michel de Notredame (Nostradamus)

In the beginning,
the end.
A shatter of stars,
alpha flares to omega.
All is nothing,
nothing, all.
Chrysalis,
close, quiet tomb,
yields the butterfly.
Seed to blossom,
bone and feather,
lava spurts orange flame.
Rock to sand,
each cell divides.
Time circles,
doubles back,
dissolves.
What was
and might have been,
and will be.
Each breath numbered,
numberless.
Cricket song,
sparrow wing.

Some hurt, some heal, some listen.

And somewhere,

someone

calls us forth

to lead us

softly

home.

A Memory of Summer

Grandpa and I walked to the woodpile.
He carried split pine
and let me hold his favorite pipe,
Grandma's gift when they were newly married.
I sat on the ground
and watched him heap the firewood high,
his back to me,
talking of other lands,
lost times he hungered to replace.
He stacked and spoke,
I silently smoked,
pretending, puffing the unlit pipe,
tobacco rich, sweet-smelling.
A snake slid from the shattered logs,
copper body gleaming.
I froze, eyes wide.
The wooden pipe dropped from my mouth
and crashed onto a rock and cracked.
The snake coiled, tongue flickering.
Grandpa turned, clutching a log.
In a flash
he smashed its shining head.
Underneath the snake exploded,
yellow, green, and dead.
Grandpa buried it,
then carefully slipped the broken pipe bowl
near his breast.

A shame about that snake, he said,
but some things can't be helped.
And some things, Grandpa added,
you just never can replace.

Glancing

Chipped teapot
in the window of the antique shop,
its handle gold and blue.
I think, *This is just like my mother's.*
I think, *This is my mother's.*
I think of that morning, the shattered cup.

For Karen Chamberlain
(December 1, 1941—September 11, 2010)

Your eyes,
bright and dark and lovely,
gaze out from the photograph—
it's an old one,
black-and-white—
and you so young and beautiful,
one hand partly covering that smile,
mischievous, mysterious.

You were so alive then,
so full of words,
so many bits of colored glass
to still be pieced together.

The truth is,
I hardly knew you.
Except that your hands shook
when you were about to step on stage,
except that your voice was quiet
when you read your poetry,
except that you seemed a frightened bird—
how could you be
a frightened bird
when you had
shaped nature,
shattered diamonds,
pounded trails,
and gentled horses?

I look into your
photograph face,
and it's as if you're
coming back
or never left
or leaping out,
your eyes aflame,
you frighten me.

I know your smile felt real.

The Day That the Lord Has Made

She wears many hats,
this woman whose name
is not Grace, but should be.
Seeing a need, she fills it.
Soup for empty bellies,
blankets
to block the cold.
Stray cats,
unwanted dogs,
she leaves them food and water.
She reaches out her hand
to all,
and smiles.
She always smiles.

Alone in her apartment,
she is looking out the window,
and she watches, watches snowflakes
disappearing as they fall.
Turning back,
she reaches out to touch
one framed photograph
encased in glass and polished brass.
Tracing patterns of faces
with a finger,
she remembers them,
long gone.

She cannot bring them back
or say where they were sent
or why.
Nor can she explain the way
that she alone survived.

Placing the frame on the kitchen table,
she seats herself opposite,
small chocolate cake between,
bright yellow candles.
Carefully, reverently,
she lights each one
and softly sings herself a wish,
then softly
sings a prayer.

Between the Lines: Visiting a Maine Cemetery, the Woman Senses Sisterhood

The stones line up neatly.
Husband, two small daughters
and, at row's end,
the woman,
Beloved in Life, Lamented in Death.
This simple carving weaves a spell
of light and shade, of subtleties,
webs of words unspoken.

She was housekeeper, he master
through their decades of devotion.
She is gone, too soon gone.
He is old, but left behind to weep
with granite to console him.
The man turns his back
to the other stone.
It stands alone
with only weeds for company.
Wife she was to him, true wife,
dam to fragile daughters.
Her years, long years
of bearing
captured in these taunting syllables,
Insane for 50 Years,
her marker reads.

"Insane," my mother muses as she stoops
to wrench a weed.
"And is it, tell me, is it any wonder?"

Same Old, Same Old

Drinking coffee in
the Golden Star diner on
Route 46,
waiting for my father.
He said he would be here.
He always says he'll be here.

Courtyard in Abiquiu, New Mexico, August 2006

Orange trumpet petals

tumble from shining vine,

corkscrew this black iron gate,

climb the adobe walls,

climb the walls,

flesh-colored walls.

The air is thick with honey,

the hummingbird cocks amber head.

Wings buzz maniacally.

Slant of saffron,

setting sun.

Gray cobblestones,

granite fountain,

iced volcano

spurts.

Small wind rises.

Five windows draped with rainbow stripes,

purple yellow blue red green.

A hand pulls back one curtain

and as quickly

lets it fall.

Trespass

He was here,

eyes reflected in the

midnight kitchen window.

But those are my eyes,

his eyes

that he gave to me,

that blinked

and I was born.

On a peg in the

hallway for 20 years,

I hang his sweater,

heavy with dust.

The photographs I burned,

but I still see him,

I can smell him.

And the moaning, when I hear it

now just means

that

upstairs

somebody is dreaming,

maybe

someone's cold.

Prophecy

The one that eats the sun has come,

sliding from the sky on a single blue thread,

reaching into Earth's belly,

fingers melting stone,

bringing forth a lump of gold

and hurling it to heaven.

Bursting and blooming

to perfect roundness,

it rises

and the one that eats the sun

follows,

ascending to black air,

mouth open,

spewing forth white glinting stars.

Untended orchard . . .

Untended orchard
I have come to eat red plums
and watch leaves falling

It Is

It is that instant of——
I don't know what.
That instant of——
why?
It is leaves——
of course, they're
orange and red and gold.
It is leaves flying across
the windshield.
It is laughter,
it is too much laughter.
It is the last warbler and
I can't follow.
It is one breath
that cannot be held.
It is that next instant,
leaves still falling,
glass breaking.
It is wind
and warbler
and
it is
almost
winter.

Late Winter Reverie

I am watching the snow come down
outside my window,
and beyond
the ponderosas,
a mist of mountain
showing itself,
then sliding into something white.
I am told it is called Twin Peaks,
but I know only that
it is vast,
stippled with fir and spruce and pine,
and where it is not
black or gray or steely green,
I know that it is white—
a crane's white wing
could not be whiter.

Here at the window,
geraniums fist
into pink snowballs
fringed with the quiet kind of green
that needs a roof and walls and light.

I know I should be working,

but the snow,

it just keeps

rising, falling,

spattering the open air,

cleaner than

a new child's breath.

And as I watch, I wonder, who

in this high place,

who then would choose to conjure,

who could want for

such a thing as spring?

Contemplative

2 a.m.
I stand
at the window.

One planet,
its light still
pure.

This dark
would be
a blessing,

if I were not
myself.
Once,

long past,
I prayed at night
by looking at the stars.

A comet
seared Your heaven.
I took comfort in its warning.

Drift

I am a burrower,
no nester,
a delver,
plunging past black
to flames molten and spearing,
the orange sparks
shooting and
scorching and
shearing,
my tunnels all melting,
with no turning back.

Still probing
and reaching,
pursuing and seeking,
not ever arriving,
just digging down deeper
past dark
into light.

Outside

Outside,
I am
looking in the window,
watching life, love, family, friends,
the everything a good home holds.

Pressing cold nose to the glass,
somehow even then
nobody sees me,
no one knows
I'm here.

Blue flames blaze
in the fireplace.
Shadows,
pillows,
beeswax candles,
polished wood and brass,
and
they are stretching hands out,
they are warm,
they, safe as
any one could be inside these fleshy shells.

My breath is wet,

it frosts the pane.

They might have just forgotten me,

forgetting they would have to first

remember.

It Is Not Things

Nansen was too kind and lost his treasure.
Truly, words have no power.
Even though the mountain becomes the sea,
Words cannot open another's mind.
                    — Zen koan

Mountain swallowed
by the sea,
but still my treasure floats
on roiling water.
Try to reel it in,
it only sinks beneath
the wave.

I used to think that
I'd gone mad.
Now that I have no doubt,
I see there's
nothing left to fear.

I must forgive
the other
for not being what
I need or want,
for being so immersed in
that small spectacle
of self.

My words do not alter
your path.
Frequently, they do not alter
mine.
My words cannot reverse
the tide
or wash one footprint
from the sand.

Open your own mind
as you choose,
and I will cook my rice.

I Haven't Met My Angel Yet
(after Emily Dickinson)

I haven't met my angel yet,
but I am sure she'd wear
a velvet gown of gold or green
and violets in her hair.
I sometimes sense her presence in
a whispered word, a breath,
a shadow on the bone-white moon,
and in her consort, Death.
For when He last approached my door,
she lingered in His shade.
Though far beyond, beyond my sight,
I, strangely unafraid,
knew she was near and let Him pass,
and so Death passed me by,
and reached, instead, He reached for her.
I heard a rush of wings, a sigh.

Let's Face It

The sunlight must fade,
so why be afraid
of night?
We cannot evade
the choices we've made—
wrong, right.
Life is a charade,
a grand masquerade,
a plight.

We cannot foresee
what's going to be.
We try.
We argue, decree,
think we have the key.
We lie.
Life's all mystery—
a sweet melody,
a sigh.

Last Moment

*I like trees because they seem more resigned to the way they have to
live than other things do.*
        — Willa Cather, *O Pioneers!*

And I, here, lying

beneath this pine,

staring up at tight green cones,

at long green needles,

one light as lime,

one dark as wooded dusk.

Now it does not concern me

what genus, what species, what name

of pine.

It is pine, that is enough.

The smell of it

new, sharp, familiar.

This earth, my bed,

so much wet stone.

I have nothing left to give

and no one to want it.

Tears, if there were,

have fallen in some distant land.

Let me say that I have been sometimes

happy.

I did the things I could. I even

did the things I dared.

A twig snaps.

Hooves, but not so near.

A squirrel——fat, red, furry——

is looking down,

one withered cone clutched

in tiny claws, its bright eyes

merely curious.

No seeds and so

the claws let go.

The cone drops

on my forehead

and

I close my eyes

and

almost laugh.

I Am (2)

I am a creature that delves in the earth,
a shaper of gems in the dark.
I am a shadow that wilts in the sun,
gray smoke floating over brown fields.
I am a river that flows to the sea,
a wave crashing onto the shore.
I am a raven that whirls in the wind,
and sings without knowing the song.
I am the dancer, or am I the dance?
I am a joker, or am I a joke?
The question unanswered, the story untold.
I am a branch that is snapped in the storm.
In the side of the world,
I'm a splinter, a thorn.

ABOUT THE AUTHOR

Lynda La Rocca was born in New York City, grew up in northern New Jersey, and is a magna cum laude graduate of Georgian Court College (now Georgian Court University), Lakewood, New Jersey. A former journalist for the *Asbury Park* (NJ) *Press*, she is employed full-time as a freelance writer and also works part-time as a teaching assistant in the Spanish/ESL laboratory at the Timberline Campus of Colorado Mountain College in Leadville, Colorado.

Her nonfiction articles, essays, and fiction have appeared in such publications as *The Denver Post, Old West, The Pueblo Chieftain, Woman's World, Delta Sky, America West Airlines Magazine, Highlights for Children*, and the *Chicago Tribune*. Her poetry has appeared in numerous state and national poetry society anthologies along with such publications as *The Wall Street Journal, The New York Quarterly, Frogpond* (Haiku Society of America), *U.S. Catholic*, and *Children's Playmate*. Her first poetry chapbook, *In the Shortness of My Days*, was published in 1993 by New Spirit Press, New York; her second poetry chapbook, *The Stillness Between*, was published in 2009 by Pudding House Publications, Ohio.

Since 2004, La Rocca has been a member of the River City Nomads, a poetry performance troupe consisting of five Colorado-based poets.

She lives in Twin Lakes, Colorado, with her husband, Steve Voynick, their dog, Luz, and an ornate box turtle named SunSpot.

CREDITS AND ACKNOWLEDGEMENTS

The following poems originally appeared in the publications listed
below:

"A Memory of Summer"
   Prize Poems 1995 (Pennsylvania Poetry Society, Inc., West
Reading, Pennsylvania; 1995)

"Late Winter Reverie"
   Encore: Prize Poems 2007 (National Federation of State Poetry
Societies, Inc., USA; 2007)

"Untended orchard . . . "
   Stanza, spring 2011 (Volume 19, No. 2, Maine Poets Society
newsletter; 2011)

"Outside"
   Colorado Central Magazine, January/February 2012 (Central
Colorado Publishing LLC, Salida, Colorado; 2012)

www.ingramcontent.com/pod-product-compliance
Lightning Source LLC
Chambersburg PA
CBHW021915040426
42447CB00007B/877